Mary McLeod Bethune

Mary McLeod Bethune

by

Eloise Greenfield

illustrated by

Jerry Pinkney

HarperCollins*Publishers*

OTHER BOOKS BY ELOISE GREENFIELD

Africa Dream
Honey, I Love and Other Love Poems
Me and Neesie
She Come Bringing Me That Little Baby Girl
Under the Sunday Tree
William and the Good Old Days
Paul Robeson
Rosa Parks
Sister
Talk About a Family
Childtimes:
A Three-Generation Memoir
With Lessie Jones Little

Mary McLeod Bethune
Text copyright © 1977 by Eloise Greenfield
Illustrations copyright © 1977 by Jerry Pinkney
All rights reserved. No part of this book may be used or reproduced in any manner whatsoever without written permission except in the case of brief quotations embodied in critical articles and reviews. Printed in the United States of America. For information address HarperCollins Children's Books, a division of HarperCollins Publishers, 10 East 53rd Street, New York, NY 10022.

Library of Congress Cataloging in Publication Data
Greenfield, Eloise
Mary McLeod Bethune.

Summary: Biography of Mary Jane McLeod Bethune who made numerous contributions to education for Afro-Americans.
1. Bethune, Mary Jane McLeod, 1875–1955—Juv. lit.   [1.Bethune, Mary Jane McLeod, 1875–1955.
2. Afro-Americans—Biography. 3. Teachers]   I. Pinkney, Jerry.   II. Title.
E185.97.B34G73   370'.92'4   [B]   [92]   76–11522
ISBN 0-690-01129-6
ISBN 0-06-446168-8(pbk.)

Mary McLeod Bethune

The sun had just come up when Mary Jane McLeod left the house with her mother and father and her brothers and sisters to go to the fields. Every morning, the whole family had to get up very early to work on the farm. But they didn't mind. The farm belonged to them. It gave them vegetables to eat and cotton to sell.

Mary knelt on the ground and pulled the weeds from around a head of cabbage. She had pulled weeds so many times before that she didn't have to think about it with her whole mind. She used part of her mind to think about her favorite dream. She thought about one day being able to read, and about having her own book and going to school.

Where Mary lived, near Mayesville, South Carolina, there were no schools for black children. She had been born there, not many years after the slaves were freed. No one in her family could read. During slavery, it had been against the law and very dangerous for anyone to teach slaves to read. Some black people had gone to secret hiding places to study and learn, but many had not been able to do that.

Mary's parents, Samuel and Patsy McLeod, had grown up as slaves, each on a different plantation. They had met and fallen in love, but they could not marry until Mr. McLeod saved enough money to buy his bride. He had to work hard all day without pay, and at night he worked to earn money. It took him many months to earn enough.

After the wedding, Mr. and Mrs. McLeod were both slaves on the same plantation. Their first fourteen children were slaves, too. They had to work on other people's farms and clean other people's houses and wash other people's clothes, all without pay. They were not happy. They wanted a place of their own where they could work and live in freedom.

Several years after the law against slavery was passed, Mr. and Mrs. McLeod were able to start their own farm. Mr. McLeod and his sons went into the woods and cut down trees to get logs. They built a four-room log cabin for the family.

Mary was born in the log cabin on July 10, 1875. She was the fifteenth child and two others were born later. Mary loved the farm. When she was very small, her father let her ride on the back of Old Bush, the mule with the bushy tail, as he pulled the plow. When she was a little older, she weeded the vegetables and picked cotton. In the house, she swept the floor and washed and shined the kerosene lamps and helped take care of the younger children.

Every morning and evening the family stood in front of the fireplace and said prayers and sang hymns together. After dinner, the children gathered around their mother as she sat in her favorite chair and told them true stories about Africa and talked about the Bible.

Listening to the stories, Mary wanted even more to be able to read. She talked about reading all the time. She told everybody in her family over and over that she didn't know how but someday she would learn to read.

One day when Mary was eleven years old, Miss Emma Wilson, a black teacher, came with the answer. She told Mary's parents that the Presbyterian Church had sent her to Mayesville to start a one-room school for black children.

Mr. and Mrs. McLeod wanted all of their children to go to school, but there was too much work to be done on the farm. Only one could go. That one, they decided, would be Mary.

On the first day of school, Mary left home early, carrying her lunch in a tin bucket. The school was

five miles away, but she was happy to walk each mile. Every step was taking her closer to something that she had wanted for a long, long time.

Miss Wilson was a good teacher and Mary was a good student. She studied hard every day, and soon she could read short words and work arithmetic problems. In the evening, she taught her family what she had learned in school. Sometimes neighbors would ask her to read their mail for them or figure out the money they should get for selling their cotton.

A few years later, Mary was graduated from Miss Wilson's school. Her parents sat with the others who had come to hear their children recite and sing on their last day there. Mary received a scholarship to Scotia Seminary, a school for black girls in Concord, North Carolina. The scholarship meant that she would not have to pay.

Mary was nervous about leaving her family for the first time and taking her first train ride. But she was excited, too. Her mother made a dress for her out of a piece of cloth that was pretty, although it wasn't new. Neighbors knitted stockings and crocheted collars as gifts. They made some of their dresses over to fit Mary.

On going-away day, her family and friends went to the train station to see her off. There was a lot of talking and laughing and kissing. They were sorry to see Mary leave, but their happiness was greater than their sadness. Mary was going off to get an education.

Scotia Seminary was a three-story brick building surrounded by grass and trees and flowers. Mary lived in a small room with two beds and two wash-stands. She had a roommate, Abbie, who became a very good friend. Later, a second brick building was added. It was named Faith Hall. Mary loved to worship in its little chapel.

Mary had classes in mathematics, languages, history, geography, and the Bible. She learned about people who lived in other countries and about people who had lived many years before. She learned about islands and oceans and mountains.

In speech class, Mary was the best student. Her strong, low voice always sounded sure, and her class-

mates listened closely to what she was saying. Her voice was also good for singing and the music teacher gave her solos.

All of the students at Scotia helped with the housework. Mary dusted and ironed and brought in coal for the fire. Much of her free time she spent in the library reading about Africa.

On graduation day, no one in her family was in the audience. They could not afford to pay the train fare. But Mary knew that they were proud of her and happy for her. She had received another scholarship, this time to Moody Bible Institute in Chicago, Illinois.

Moody Bible Institute would teach Mary to be a missionary. She believed in the Christian religion and wanted other people to believe in it, too. She wanted to teach Christianity, especially in Africa. People in Africa and other parts of the the world have their own religions. But Mary thought that hers was best.

Mary and other students at Moody were sent out to visit prisoners in the jail and people who were sick or without money. The students read the Bible to them

page 16 b

and prayed and sang hymns. They also helped other people whenever they could and invited them to come to the school for church services. Mary and five other students traveled to other states to start Sunday schools. They rode in a train coach called "The Gospel Car."

By the time Mary finished her work at Moody, she had grown up. She was a woman now, rather large, with smooth, dark skin. She had learned all that Moody could teach and was ready to be a missionary. But she had a very unpleasant surprise. She could find no openings for a black missionary in Africa.

Mary went home to Mayesville. During the years that she was in school, she had not often been able to return home, and she was glad to see her family. But she was disappointed to have to go back home without the job she had studied so hard for. She helped Miss Wilson in Mayesville School until she got a job as a teacher at Haines Institute in Augusta, Georgia.

Haines had been started by Lucy Laney, who had once been a slave. Miss Laney was still in charge of the school. She never seemed to get tired of helping her students and the teachers who worked for her. She always had new ideas to make Haines better. Watching her, Mary soon forgot her disappointment and put all of herself into being the best teacher that she could be.

Most of what Mary earned she sent home to her family. She helped to pay for the education of her younger sisters and to buy her parents a new home. Their old one had burned down.

A few years after she began teaching, Mary met Albertus Bethune, also a teacher, who became her husband. The following year, their son, Albert, was born.

When Albert was five years old, Mary Bethune made a big decision. She wanted to start a school of her own. She thought of Miss Laney and Miss Wilson, and she remembered herself as a child longing to learn. There were many black children like her who lived in places without schools. They had questions but no answers. They wanted to learn and she wanted to teach them.

She heard about Daytona Beach, Florida, where a new railroad was being built. The workmen who were putting down the railroad track were not being paid enough. They lived with their families in camps that were too crowded. There were no schools. Mrs. Bethune decided that she would go there.

When Mrs. Bethune arrived in Daytona Beach, she had only one dollar and fifty cents. She stayed with a friend, and every day she went for a walk, looking for a building that she could use as a school. Finally, she found an old two-story cottage. The owner said he would rent it to her for eleven dollars a month. He agreed to wait a few weeks until she could raise the first month's rent.

Mrs. Bethune visited the homes of black families, telling them about her school. Neighbors came to paint the cottage and to fix the broken steps. Children helped with the cleaning.

On an autumn day in 1904, Mrs. Bethune stood in the doorway of the cottage, smiling and ringing a bell. It was time for school to start. Five little girls came in and took their seats. The school was named

the Daytona Normal and Industrial School for Girls. It was an elementary school, and Albert would learn there, too, until he was older.

Mrs. Bethune and the students used wooden boxes as desks and chairs. They burned logs and used the charcoal as pencils. They mashed berries and used the juice as ink.

The children loved the school. Some of them lived there with Mrs. Bethune. All of them wanted to help raise money for the rent and for the books and paper and lamps and beds that they needed.

After classes, they made ice cream and pies to sell. The children peeled and mashed sweet potatoes while Mrs. Bethune rolled the crust. They gave programs at hotels and in churches. The children sang and recited. Mrs. Bethune spoke to the audiences about the school. She bought a secondhand bicycle and rode all over Daytona Beach, knocking on doors and asking people for their help.

Many people gave. Some of them were rich, and some of them did not have much money themselves but were willing to share the little that they had.

When too many children wanted to attend and a larger building was needed, adults in the community again gave their time and work. They took away the trash from the land that Mrs. Bethune bought. Those who were carpenters helped to put the building up. Those who were gardeners planted flowers and trees around it.

Mrs. Bethune named the new building Faith Hall in honor of her favorite building at Scotia Seminary. She had faith in God, in herself, and in black people. Over the door she hung a sign that said "Enter to learn."

Across from Faith Hall, Mrs. Bethune started a small farm. The students planted fruits and vegetables to use and to sell. They grew strawberries, tomatoes, string beans, carrots, and corn. They grew sugar cane to make syrup.

As the years passed, more students came to the school, and more teachers. More buildings were added. Albert went away to school, but Mrs. Bethune was busier than ever. Almost every day a new problem arose that she had to solve.

One day, a student became very ill. Because there was no hospital for blacks for many, many miles, Mrs. Bethune rushed her to the nearest white hospital. The doctors agreed to take care of her, but not inside the hospital. They put the patient on the back porch with a screen around her bed.

Mrs. Bethune was very angry, but there was nothing she could do. The student was too sick to be moved to another hospital. But when the girl was well, Mrs. Bethune decided that someone had to start a hospital for blacks in Daytona Beach, and she would do it. She started a little two-bed hospital which later had twenty beds. She named it McLeod Hospital in memory of her father, who had died. It saved many black lives.

Later that same year, one of Mrs. Bethune's brothers came for his first visit. He walked around the campus with his sister and visited classrooms where young people were being taught to use their minds and their hands. The choir sang for him. He was proud of his sister and of all that he saw and heard, and Mrs. Bethune was proud to show him what had been done.

The school that had started as an elementary school for girls became a high school, then a junior college, and finally a college. It joined with a men's college and was given a new name—Bethune-Cookman College—with Mrs. Bethune as president. It had the only library for black people in that part of Florida.

Mrs. Bethune did not spend all of her time at the school. She joined groups of people who were working for the rights of black men, women, and children. She wrote articles for newspapers and magazines. She traveled across the United States making speeches about the need for public schools, jobs, houses, and food. She became famous for her devotion to black youth. The sureness in her voice and her slow, careful way of speaking became well known.

For many years Mrs. Bethune had suffered with asthma. It sometimes made her very sick. She had to struggle for breath. Doctors had told her that she needed more rest. But she said that she had to work until every black boy and girl had a chance for an education. She remembered their African heritage,

and hers. "The drums of Africa still beat in my heart," she said. "They will not let me rest."

In the 1920's and 1930's, the United States was in great trouble. There were millions of people without jobs. Some of them starved. Many young people had to stop going to school.

Mrs. Bethune was asked by President Franklin D. Roosevelt to live in Washington, D.C., and work with the National Youth Administration. She did not want to leave her school, but she knew that she was needed for this special job. She moved to Washington and was in charge of finding jobs for young blacks all over the country. She visited many states and talked to these young people about their problems.

After eight years, she returned to her home on the campus of Bethune-Cookman. Not many years later, Mrs. Bethune had to stop working. She was sick more often and her heart was weak.

Mary McLeod Bethune had spent her life working for others. She had started the National Council of Negro Women. She had been president of the Association for the Study of Negro Life and History,

working with Dr. Carter G. Woodson to make known the true history of black people. She had worked with many groups of blacks and women and teachers and church members. The walls of her study were covered with awards and medals that had been presented to her.

Now her hair was white and she was tired, though she was careful not to show her tiredness and continued to give advice when it was needed. But most of the time she stayed at home, enjoying the visits of her son and grandchildren and great-grandchildren, and of the many other people who came to see her.

Sometimes Mrs. Bethune took her cane and went for a very slow walk. She walked across the campus of her school, looking at the hundreds of students and the buildings and lawns and remembering how it all had started.

In 1955 at the age of seventy-nine, Mary McLeod Bethune died of a heart attack. She was buried on the grounds of the school she loved.

In her will Mrs. Bethune left a message for black people. She said that they must believe in themselves and help each other. She said that it is through learning that children grow up to be strong men and women. She said that children must never stop wanting to build a better world.

On a hot summer day, nineteen years after Mrs. Bethune's death, thousands of people gathered in a park in Washington, D.C. They had come to honor her memory. They watched as the large cloth covering a tall statue was lifted for the first time.

The statue is of Mrs. Bethune. She is handing her will to a girl and a boy. Some of the words from the will are written on the base of the statue. People from all over the world go to Washington to visit the park. Children like to play there. They run close to the statue and walk all the way around it to read the last words of Mary McLeod Bethune: "I leave you faith, I leave you hope, I leave you love."